THE SONG TURNING BACK INTO ITSELF

BOOKS BY AL YOUNG

Dancing
Snakes
The Song Turning Back Into Itself

The Song Turning Back Into Itself

POEMS

BY AL YOUNG

HOLT, RINEHART AND WINSTON
New York Chicago San Francisco

Most of these poems (some in slightly different form) have already
appeared in the following publications: **Alas** (Buenos Aires),
**Aldebaran Review, The Anthology, Black Dialogue, Black on Black,
Brilliant Corners, Camels Coming, Chicago Review, Crystalline Flight,
Dices, El Corno Emplumado** (Mexico City), **Essence, 100 Flowers, Galley
Sail Review, Guabi, Hanging Loose, Illuminations, The Lit, Loveletter,
Natural Process, Perspectives, Rogue River Gorge, Sponge, 23 California
Poets, Works.**

"Trbute" and "Everywhere" were first published in the **Chicago Review;** "Yes,
the Secret Mind Whispers" in **Hanging Loose;** "The Prestidigitator (2)" and
"Identities" in **Rogue River Gorge;** "Dear Old Stockholm," "There Is a
Sadness," "Ponce de Leon," "The Kiss," portions of "The Song Turning Back
Into Itself," and "Malaguena Salerosa" in **Natural Process** published by
Hill and Wang. "The Curative Powers of Silence" and "One West Coast"
appears courtesy of The Phillip Perry Co.
Grateful acknowledgment is made for use of the following: A passage from
The Pillow Book of Sei Shonagon, translated by Arthur Waley. Used by
permission of George Allen and Unwin Ltd. One haiku from **Twentieth
Century Poetry** by Kai-yu Hsu. Copyright © 1963 by Kai-yu Hsu. Reprinted
by permission of Doubleday and Company, Inc. Two lines from Blaise
Cendrars, **Selected Writings,** © 1968 by Walter Albert. Reprinted by
permission of New Directions Publishing Corporation.

Published simultaneously in Canada by Holt, Rinehart
and Winston of Canada, Limited.

ISBN Hardbound: 0-03-086692-8
ISBN Paperback: 0-03-086693-6

Library of Congress Catalog Card Number: 74-155542

First Edition

Designer: Betty Binns
Printed in the United States of America

For Franchot Young,
superb pianist & brother;
for Billy, Richard, Walter, Monte, Aveda
& for Arl

Contents

LONELINESS

I don't know if you have been away,
I go to bed with you, & I wake up with you.
In my dreams you are beside me.
If the earrings of my ears tremble
I know it is you moving in my heart.

Nahuatl Indian Song/Poem
(Mexico)

The poet is the dreamer.
He dreams that the clock stops
& 100 angels wandering wild
drift into his chamber
where nothing has been settled

Should he get himself photographed
seated next to a mountain
like Chairman Mao
the real sun flashing golden
off his real eyes
like the light off stones
by oceans?

Give me your perfect hand
& touch me simply with a word,
one distillation of forever

Should he put his white tie on
with his black shirt
& pass himself off as a docile gangster
for the very last time?

The poet's dream is real
down to the last silver bullet

Should he slip again to Funland
in the city & throw dimes down holes
to watch hungry women flicker
one hair at a time
in kodacolor
from sad civilized boxes?

Should he practice magic
on politicians &
cause them to crack their necks
in a laughing fit?

The poet is the dreamer.
He dreams babies asleep in wombs
& counts the wasted sighs
lost in a flake of dusty semen
on a living thigh

Should he dream the end of an order
the abolition of the slave trade,
the restoration to life
of dead millions
filing daily past time clocks
dutifully gorging themselves
on self-hatred & emptiness?

Should he even dream
an end to loneliness,
the illusion that

we can do without
& have no need
of one another?

It is true that he needs you,
I need you,
I need your pain & magic,
I need you now more than ever
in every form & attitude—
gesturing with a rifle in your hand
starving in some earthly sector
or poised in heavenly meditation
listening to the wind
with the third ear
or staring into forever
with the ever-watchful third eye,
you are needed

The poet is the dreamer &
the poet is himself the dream
& in this dream
he shares your presence

Should he smash down walls
& expose the ignorance
beneath our lying noisiness?

No! No!
the gunshot he fires
up into the silent air
is to awaken

Floating thru morning
    I arrive at afternoon
& see the bright lightness
    light ness
    of it all

& thank God
& go on living
taking spoiled strawberries
& a tapioca pudding gone bad
    out the ice box

Must wash my hair &
    go get it cut off my head
    head itches
Notice my luck changes
    when I've had
    a hair cut
same as if I dont rise before noon
    the day doesnt go right

Afternoon becomes evening becomes night

There're worlds into worlds between all worlds
    so dont worry
    about divisions of day

for even when I fall out asleep the day
        wont have ended
        wont have begun

In fact years whoosh by in time for me
        to see myself as endless fool child
& to learn better than
        to laugh at such conditions

Now I bathe & go out into the streets
        airplane raging overhead
        (your head perhaps)
        reminding me how
        even floating must come to an end

I first saw you in a trance
(you were in the trance, not me).
Me I was dancing

on turbulent waters.
All my shores had been pulled up
& naked I was nowhere

but there was some drowsy grace you offered,
some rendezvous from way-back to be fulfilled.
I moved toward you

saying everything,
you nothing.
The 20th century moon

did its turn-around,
revealing how much the sun it was
in the face of your light,

all that light,
in the daytime,
at night

The Old Fashioned Cincinnati Blues

for Jesse "Lone Cat" Fuller

O boy the blues!
I sure do love blues
but the blues dont like me

This is Cincinnata Ohia 1949
& that's me & my brother Frank
in the NY Central Train Station
trying to get it together
on our way down
to Meridian Mississippi
where later I hid
in cornfields, smoked butts &
dreamed all about
the sunny grownup future,
dreamed about Now

Ah but that Now that
Right Now that is,
all I wanna dream about's
that NY Cincy Terminal
that summer with its intervals
of RC Cola Coolers,
tin tub baths taken
one at a time
back behind the evening stove—

Chickens—

Our grandmother
(Mrs Lillian Campbell)—

Cousin George & Uncle John
swapping ghost stories
Saturday nite—

O Americana!
United Statesiana!

A lonesome high,
a funnytime cry,
the blues
the blues
the blues

The Problem of Identity

Used to identify with my father   first   making me want to be a
   gas station attendant   simple   drink coca-cola   listen to
   the radio, work on people's cars, hold long conversations in
   the night   black   that clean gas smell of oil & no-gas,
   machine coolness, rubber, calendars, metal sky, concrete, the
   bearing of tools, the wind—true Blue labor Red & White

Identified with Joe Louis: Brown Bomber, you know   They'd pass
   along the mud streets of Laurel Mississippi in loud speaker
   truck, the white folks, down by where the colored schools was
   & all of us, out there for Recess or afterschool are beck-
   oned to come get your free picture of Joe Louis, *C'mon &
   get it kids it's Free, c'mon naow*—What it is is chester-
   field cigarettes   in one corner of the beautiful slick photo of
   Mr. Louis is the blurb, *Joe like to smoke too, see, and he
   want all yall to follow right long in his footsteps & buy
   up these here chesterfields & smoke your little boodies
   off & youll be able to step up in that ring begloved &
   punch a sucker out.*   It was the glossiness of the photo, I
   finally figured out years later, that had me going—didnt
   really matter whose picture was on it altho it was nice to've
   been Joe's because he was about as great as you could get
   downsouth, post world war II as the books say

Identified with Otis (think his name was)   worked at grocery
   store in Ocean Springs, came by, would sit & draw on pieces

of brown paperbag, drew in 1940s style of cartoons bordering on "serious" sketching, i.e., in the manner of those sultan cartoons with the harem gals by that black cartoonist Sims you see em all the time in old Esquires & Playboys Well, that's the way Otis could draw & he'd show me in the make-do livingroom seated on do-fold how to do a portrait of a chic perfect anglo-featured woman, say, in profile out of his head built mostly from magazine & picture-show impressions, & he could draw lots of world things, drew me for instance

Later Otis went up to Chicago, sadness, madness, wed, bled, dope, hopeless, catapulted into the 20th century like the rest of us—rudely,
                    steeped in homemade makeshift chemical bliss of/or flesh, waiting for nothing less than The Real Thing

Pachuta, Mississippi / A Memoir

I too
once lived
in the country

Incandescent
fruits
in moonlight
whispered to me
from trees
of
1950
swishing
in the green nights

wavelengths away
from
tongue-red meat
of melon

wounded squash
yellow as old afternoons

chicken
in love
with calico

hiss & click of flit gun

juice music
    you suck up
lean stalks of field cane

            Cool as sundown
            I lived there too

For JoAnne in Poland

You are not to trouble yourself
with your ladyness
your blackness,
mysteries
of having been brought up
on collard greens
        bagels
            &
            Chef Boy-Ar-Dee

Nor must you let the great haters
of our time
rattle in your heart

They are small potatoes
whose old cries
for blood
may be heard
any afternoon of the millennium
any portion
        of this
                schoolroom globe

How quickly morphology
    shifts
        the whole landscape
    thrice uprooted
        all the tall redwoods
    yanked & shipped to Japan
        since you snapped
            that one

My eyes grow new
        the smile crookeder—
            Here your coloring
    shines out of you differently
        as tho measured thru
    some other kind of prism
            one by which the wavelength
                of a smile
            is easily recorded

Like distant hills by moonlight
        your own dark beauty
            brightens
        like meanings of remembered places
            illuminated
                by time & distance

Carmel Valley
the Zoo at the end
of the Judah line
Tomales Bay
McGee Street
Smith Grade Road
Avenida Cinco de Mayo
Guadalajara Guadalajara
the beach at Point Reyes of
saying goodbye
to sand the ocean the untakeable
sea breeze
doorway
backyard
garden
alleyway
bench
forest of countryside & city

The passing of time'll
shatter your heart
recorded in
mute shadow & light
the photographer's hour

THE SONG TURNING BACK
INTO ITSELF

I sing folk tunes unrhymed.
With my heart keeping the beat,
Trust your sorrow, then, to my bosom
Where it will find its cure.

Li Chin-fa

The Song Turning Back Into Itself 1

Breathing in morning
breezing thru rainbows
vanishing in my own breath mist,
how can I still not feel
this warm beat of beats
my own heart of hearts,

myself: an articulate colored boy
who died lucky
who wouldve kept talking himself
into dying,
creatively of course,
the soulful touch
pulsing thru his nervous system
like light thru the arteries of trees,

that mystified young man
whose stupidity knew no bounds
& at whose touch
gold shriveled to tinfoil
wine gurgled into faucet water,

a firstclass fuckup
who but for divine mercy
would have gone

out of commission
long ago
would have become
the original loveboat
cracked up against rocks
in fog or funk,

the rocks in his hard nappy head
the fog in his big blind eyes
the funk in his & everyone's blood
held in
waiting,

waiting

The Song Turning Back Into Itself 2

A song for little children

Always it's either
a beginning
or some end:
the baby's being born
or its parents are
dying, fading on
like the rose
of the poem
withers, its light going out
while gardens come in
to bloom

Let us stand on streetcorners
in the desolate era
& propose a new kind
of crazyness

Let us salute one another
one by one
two by two
the soft belly
moving toward
the long sideburns
the adams apple
or no apple at all

Let there be
in this crazyness
a moon
a violin
a drum

Let the beautiful brown girl
join hands with
her black sister
her golden sister
her milkskinned sister
their eternal wombs
turning with the moon

Let there be a flute
to squeal above
the beat & the bowing
to open us up
that the greens
the blues
the yellows
the reds
the silvers &
indescribable rusts
might flow out
amazingly
& blend
with the wind

Let the wobbly spin
of the earth
be a delight

wherein
a caress forms
the most perfect circle

Let the always be love
the beginning be love
love the only
possible
end

Ocean Springs Missippy
you dont know about that
unless youve died in magnolia
tripped across the Gulf
& come alive again
or fallen in the ocean
lapping up light
like the sun digging
into the scruffy palm leaves
fanning the almighty trains
huffing it choo-choo
straight up our street
morning noon & nighttrain
squalling that moan
like a big ass blues man
smoking up the sunset

Consider the little house
of sunken wood
in the dusty street
where my father would
cut his fingers
up to his ankles
in fragrant coils
of lumber shavings
the backyard of nowhere

Consider Nazis & crackers
on the same stage
splitting the bill

Affix it all to
my memory of Ma
& her love of bananas
the light flashing
in & out of our lives
lived 25¢ at a time
when pecans were in season
or the crab & shrimp
was plentiful enough
for the fishermen
to give away for gumbo
for a soft hullo
if you as a woman
had the sun in your voice
the wind over your shoulder
blowing the right way
at just that moment in history

I violinize peace
in the Nazi era;
semen-colored doves
perched atop sea trains
from the decks of which
women are singing
anti-death songs;
magnificent birds
flap in & out
of tonal pictures
before disappearing
into the green
the blue
the rolling white
of an oceanic music

Tipping thru this skylight
along rooftops
to snuggle in
quaintly
with paintable pigeons
I can still feel
the red & white
the blood sonata
cello'd from me

bow against bone
finger pluck of flesh
as
    I
      laugh
            colors
into your warm wet mouth

          •

Behold dogcatchers
the lady watchers
the simple twist of hip
as it cuts electric air
bringing endless delight

I would walk you up trees
& inscribe at the tops
in leaves
these very words
Let us change the design
of their celluloid architecture
into a shape where love could live
(in street Spanish & Swahili)

          •

This music is real

Feel the rhythm

the lips

Feel today

vibrating

in the throat

Feel sound

Feel space

O feel the presence of

light

brighter than distant circuses

in the child night

of the soul

The Song Turning Back Into Itself 5

The song skips around
The song jumps
like a little boy
leaps a mud puddle

I park in rainlight
I run out of rhymes
I splash thru the puddle
I land in a change
for 10 years seem like
water be rolling
off my back
one bead at a time
but with light
in the center of
every single one

The song sings new images
variations on the theme
of human love &
its shadow
loneliness
(Billie Holiday
mightve been busy
feeding on nuances &

loving a man but
she wouldve understood,
understanding being
the only honorable escape
in the end)

Sing me shadows
Sing me puddles
Sing me rain
Sing me holidays & nights
Sing me holiness
Sing me loneliness
Sing me a skip & a jump
    across a thousand years

But dont sing love,

    just signal

The Song Turning Back Into Itself 6

Terrestrial blues

Again
who am I?
Certainly not the boy
I started out to be
nor the man
nor the poet

Sometimes
alone & saddened
(which is to say joyous)
I get glimpses of myself
the eternal spirit
floating from flower
to tree to grasshopper,
thru whole herds of cattle

I become the skies,
the very air itself—
Me: all things
Me: nothing

It would confuse me
if I didnt know
these lbs. of meat
bearing the name

my people gave me
to be simply
every body's condition

My soul
knows no name,
no home in being

My soul
seeks your soul

Let us laugh
each at the other
& be friends

The fly-away song

Get that feeling sometimes
that
you-cant-hold-me-down
feeling

Wanna shatter
into
ten thousand fragments of emotion—

Splinter!

Rise
above this quivering concrete world
& go sailing thru beds & minds

Sail
higher
&
HIGHER

Crazy that way

SING
one sweet long song to undo
all sickness & suffering

down there on the ground . . .
one huge human gust of insight
& forgiveness

SOARING
over rooftops with
Chagall's chickens

ALIVE

WAKING!

THE PRESTIDIGITATOR

What you gonna do when they burn your barrelhouse down?
What you gonna do when they burn your barrelhouse down?
Gonna move out the piano & barrelhouse on the ground.

Traditional Afro-American Blues

A prestidigitator makes things disappear,
vanish, not unlike a well-paid bookkeeper
or tax consultant or champion consumer

The poet is a prestidigitator, he makes
your old skins disappear & re-clothes you
in sturdy raiment of thought, feeling, soul,

dream & happenstance. Consider him villain of
the earthbound, a two-fisted cowboy with
pencil in one hand & eraser in the other

dotting the horizon of your heart with cool
imaginary trees but rubbing out more than he
leaves in for space so light can get thru

I draw hats on rabbits, sew women back
together, let fly from my pockets flocks of
vibratory hummingbirds. The things Ive got

up my sleeve would activate the most listless
of landscapes (the cracked-earth heart of a bigot,
say) with pigeons that boogaloo, with flags that

light up stabbed into the brain. Most of all it's
enslaving mumbo-jumbo that I'd wipe away, a trick
done by walking thru mirrors to the other side

Mayakovsky was right
The brass of my tuba does blacken
as I oompah & twist down nights

even the best female poets
couldnt brighten with song,
a quiet dog barking distantly

my only excuse for being alive
so late past 12 by taxi
horn & radio in the rain

finally having made it
to the middle of nowhere
toes aching from the walk

but fingers intact & head
quite nicely on some other planet
where there're no tempting images

to soften the Indian in me,
no sudden left turns or halts
on roads not marked for traffic,

my women human beings being human
who touch my body with a silence
that electrifies like poetry

Mexico, 1969

Suddenly
I touch upon wordlessness,
I who watch Cheryl
the blind girl who lives up the street
walking at night
when she thinks no one's looking
deliberately heading into hedges & trees
in order to hug them
& to be kissed,
thus are we each
hugged & kissed.

Wordless
I fill up
listening for nothing
for nothing at all

as when in so-called life
I am set shivering with warmth
by a vision
with the eyes closed
of the Cheryl in me
when I think no one's looking,
plopped down in a field of grass
under watchful trees

letting the pre-mind dream
of nothing at all
nothing at all
no flicker
no shadow
no voice
no cry,

not even dreaming

—being dreamed

Yes, The Secret Mind Whispers

for Bob Kaufman

Poetry's a tree
forever at your door
neither scratching nor
knocking but everywhere
eager to force its way
into the soft warm room
of your ornery old heart,
   slipping
    its fat pink tongue
       into sensitive linings
    of your weary young ear

A tree bearing blossoms, a flower
surfacing in a canal of blood,
the dream auto with dream motor
that idles eternally but has
no moving parts, no fumes just
fragrances beneficial to breathe

It breathes mystery this tree
    but no more so
   than moons over midnight seas
or the breast of a woman/child
    to whom menstruation's happening
      for the first time

It's the practice of yoga
  on rainy nights in cities,
    the sudden thought of death
      halfway thru dessert, a
  magic wafer you take
      into your mouth
          &
  swallow for dear life

Sunday Illumination

Ive found peace & it's good sleeping late today—head full of
eternal ideas, eternal emptiness; Phil Elwood jazz on KPFA,
my wife sunny in tattered red skirt & sea blue T shirt on
back yard grass getting her Spanish lesson

"How would I say: Friday I went to a party & heard some good
gospel music?"—& I try to explain the preterite & the im-
perfect perfectly WHEW! but keep interrupting her with
poems & to watch a young bee zero in on flaming fuchsia
branches, wondering if flower & insect survive ex-lives

Then we go hiking in the Berkeley hills first time all year since
Europe, marriage, satori in the slums—New houses have
sprung up, split-level clutter; a half finished trap is going up
on the spot top of Dwight Way where we'd sit on a pile of
lumber for panoramic vista of Berkeley Oakland Alcatraz in
the Bay & dazzling San Francisco in the sun—What was it
like here before the invasions?

So by now I got to pee & head aches from heat & climb & hot-
dogs we bought & ate walking for breakfast, foul fare—no
place to sit—Some affluent dogs in heat trail us round a
bend—the old motorcycle trail looks dangerously uninter-
esting, guys go up there scrambling & fall—My shirt's
sticking to my sweat & the friends we thought we'd drop in
on, whatve we to say to them after all?

Descending Arden Steps I make water on a bush, she covering for me—humorous taboo—then comes our pause on the stone bench where we almost ruled out wedlock that torturous fall twilight of long ago Campanile carrillon woe

Time to count our blessings as in my heart all pain ceases & for the longest moment all day I see my sad funny self on earth & the gentle terror of her female soul, beautiful, but we're alive NOW accumulating karma, no time to hide in places —no place to hide in time.

Some old Mexico Lisbon set
rainy at night & shimmery.
I alone flop around in midnight,
see everything from angel angle.

New moonless couples mourn by
arm in arm & all hands
after evenings of being quiet,
for soon whatever's to happen's

happened already, always has.
I smile out over the situation
to keep their tears to myself,
tired of time & so much in need of

this mirage of lovers parading.
Safe, I can sense that I'm soon to
awake with no possible camera
to record what I just saw asleep

It's time the clock got thrown out the window
& the difference between waking & sleeping
be left undeclared, unassumed.
                              It's the
heart's turn to do a few spins in its fluid.

It's time the birds that play in the street
(that you had to slow down for this morning)
flew into your machine & introduced themselves.

It's time you silenced the radio, the stereo,
the TV, the tea kettle, the kettle drum &
flew to where the inner ear beckons, where
closed eyes have always tingled to take you,
to the end of space if necessary, to the place
the horizon's always promised, to a glowing
spirit world where you'd as soon eat as not,
as soon drink as not, as soon make love as not,
as soon be water as air, as soon be moon as sun.

It's time you made yourself beautiful again,
spreading like color in every direction,
rising & rising to every occasion.
                              Summer
may be coming in, maybe not, this painful year.

Spring is the thing that your window frames now.

It's time you soaked in the new light & laughed.

Evening isnt so much a playland as it is
a rumpus room, a place where harmony
isnt always complementary & where
spaces between palmtrees of the heart
arent always so spread out.

By 3 A.M.
there's love in her hose for the sailor
of saxophones or guitars & she'll try & take
the whole night into her skilled mouth
as tho that were the lover she really wanted
to rub against when all the time true love
inhabits her own fingernails & unshaven body.

You love her for the mental whore she is,
the clothed sun in Libra, the horny sister
who with her loose hair flying can get
no better attention for the time being

EVERYWHERE

One West Coast

for Gordon Lapides

Green is the color of everything
that isnt brown, the tones ranging
like mountains, the colors changing.

You look up toward the hills & fog—
the familiarity of it after so many years
   a resident tourist.

          A young man walks
toward you in vague streetcrossing denims
& pronounced boots. From the pallor of
   his gait, the orange splotch twin gobs of sunset
   in his shades, from the way he vibrates
   his surrounding air, you can tell, you can tell
     he's friendly, circulating,

       he's a Californian: comes to visit,
     stays for years, marries, moves a wife in,
   kids, wears out TV sets, gets stranded on
          loneliness,
      afternoon pharmaceutica,
    so that the sky's got moon in it by
     B o'clock, is blooo, is blown—

        The girls: theyre all
    winners reared by grandmothers & CBS.

Luckier ones get in a few dances with
mom, a few hours, before dad goes back
in the slam, before "G'bye I'm off
to be a singer!" & another runaway
Miss American future drifts
over the mountain &
into the clouds.

Still
there's a beautifulness about California.
It's based on the way each eyeblink toward
the palms & into the orange grove leads backstage
into the onionfields.

Unreachable, winter happens inside you.

Your unshaded eyes dilate at the spectacle.

You take trips to contain the mystery.

How much of me is sandwiches radio beer?
How much pizza traffic & neon messages?
I take thoughtful journeys to supermarkets,
philosophize about the newest good movie,
camp out at magazine racks & on floors,
catch humanity leering back in laundromats,
invent shortcuts by the quarter hour

There's meaning to all this itemization
& I'd do well to look for it in woodpiles
& in hills & springs & trees in the woods
instead of staying in my shack all the time
thinking too much,
                    falling asleep in old chairs

All those childhood years spent in farmhouses
& I still cant tell one bush from another—
Straight wilderness would wipe me out
faster than cancer from smoking cigarettes

My country friends are out all day long
stomping thru the woods all big-eyed &
that's me walking the road afternoons,
head in some book,
            all that hilly sweetness wasting

                            Late January
                            Sonoma Mountain Road
                            in the Year of the Dragon

How overwhelming
that Lester tune
heard just out of the rain
early one night
in a café bar
full of African students
midtown Madrid
September 1963
young & dumb & lonesome
a long ways from home
amazed at my tall
cheap rum & coke
patting the wetness
from my leathered foot
to that Lester tune
cut by Cozy Cole
blown from a jukebox
right up the street from where
Quixote's Cervantes once died

I Arrive in Madrid

The wretched of the earth
are my brothers.
Neither priest
nor state
nor state of mind
is all God is
who must understand
to have put up for so long
with my drinking & all my restlessness
my hot & cold running around
unwired
to any dogma;
the way I let the eyes
of dark women
in southern countries
rock my head
like a translucent vessel
in turbulent waters.

Long have I longed for adventure,
a peculiar kind of romance
on the high seas of this planet.
Victimized at last
I float alone
exploring time

in search of tenderness,
a love
with no passage attached.

So this is dictatorship,
a watery monday morning
smell of the atlantic
still blowing thru me.
If you have ever died or been born
you will understand
when I speak of everything being salty
like the taste of my mother's tears
when I came back to earth
thru her
after much of the bombing & blood-letting
had taken place here
when Spain was the name of some country
she knew from the words of some popular song
publicized over the radio.

This city too
feels as tho it's held together by publicity
but publicity is going to lose its power
over the lives of men
once we have figured out just what within us
is more powerful & more beautiful
than program or text.

For now
there is language & Spanish to cope with,
there are eyelashes & chromosomes
pesetas pounds francs & dollars
& a poverty even wine cannot shut out.

Malagueña Salerosa

for Roberto Mates & for Doris

What beautiful eyes youve got there
underneath your own two eyebrows
underneath your own two eyebrows
what beautiful eyes youve got there

That's Mexican for O youre too much!
I always loved that mariachi song,
learned it on the Three Gold Star Bus
runs out of ratty Tijuana on out
thru dusty Sonora where they stop you
for no reason to search your bags
as if to ask that you promise you wont
do poems about simply what happens,
on up to Michoacán my green Indian dream
to the top of it all—Mexico D.F.

There one night in the big city
Bob & I were happy & fantastic
tripping up Calle Shakespeare,
bourgeois part of town with maids,
arm in arm with joyous Doris
stuck on her NYC politician lover,
Bob brooding his Havana heaven,
me so sad for my only California

We molest a *macho* a jitterbug—
"How far's it from here to Yucatán?"
"Ay hombre as far as I am dronk!"
—only so much kinder in Spanish spoken

Then the four of us arms all linked
danced all the way to quiet Michelet
to serenade young Lady D. goodnight

This Mexico City's vanished.
Bob's back in Detroit working welfare.
Doris whoever she was is no more.
There isnt any such jitterbug drunk.
The me of then is gone forever

Good thing the song's still around

Joy/Spring

All dream, all whim
(not necessarily yours either)

—these fields of Jalisco
the flowery dungsmell

sweet organic smell of
burro & milkcow

A mustache rises into the air
where it's morning always,

widows crunching on popsicle
pat fat tortilla balls.

A man is wobbling
up the road

half drunk with presence
& knowing for sure

some peace that's a preview
of what's waiting for us all.

"Wait your turn!"
his happy eyes sing.

"Wait your turn!"
the tortilla woman pat.

Joy gives him reason
to smile in this season

& it's all dream,
dreamers

Ponce de León / A Morning Walk

You too if you work hard enough
can end up being the name of a street
in a drowsy little Indian town
a day's drive from Mexico City
where orphans like bold Joselito
hustle in the taxi burro streets,
where cosmetic fragrances mingle
with scents of ripe & overripe fruits
& vegetables, where the smell of breakfast
& dinner are almost the same.

The natural odor of dung & bodysweat
rises from the zócalo into a sky, semi-
industrialized, housing the spirits of
blue señoritas with sun soaking into
their rain-washed skirts dried dustier
& wrinklier than red or green pepper.

While a crazy rooster's crowing late
a brown baby delights in orange & yellow
balloons floating up like laughter
to tenement windows where a whole family
of older kids wave happy soap wands
that yield fat bubbles part air part
water part light that pop in the faces

of prickly straw behatted gents
rambling by below, ragged & alive—

One morning's moment in this ageless
stone thoroughfare named after just one
dead Spaniard who wanted to live forever

Moon Watching by Lake Chapala

*I love to cross a river in very
bright moonlight and see the
trampled water fly up in chips
of crystal under the oxen's feet.*

The Pillow Book of Sei Shōnagon,
10th Century

IT CAN BE beautiful this sitting by oneself all alone except for
the world, the very world a literal extension of living leaf, surface
& wave of light: the moon for example. American poet Hazel Hall
felt,

"I am less myself
& more of the sun"

which I think upon these cool com-
mon nights being at some remove, in spirit at least, from where
they are busy building bombs & preparing concentration camps
to put my people into; I am still free to be in love with dust &
limbs (vegetable & human) & with lights in the skies of high
spring.

IN THE AFTERNOON you watch fishermen & fisherboys in
mended boats dragging their dark nets thru the waters. You
can even buy a little packet of dried sardines like I do, a soda,
& lean against the rock & iron railings but you wont be able to
imagine the wanderings of my own mustachio'd dad who was a

fisherman in Mississippi in the warm streams of the Gulf of Mexico. How time loops & loops! Already I'm drunk with the thought of distances. I do that look skyward & re-chart the constellations. No one to drop in on. No one to drop in on me. It's been a long time since I've had nothing better to do than establish myself in one spot & stare directly into the faces of the moon, the golden orange white brown blue moon, & listen to the tock of my heart slowing down in the silence. I can almost hear in the breeze & picture in the sniffable award-winning moonlight the doings & dyings of my hard-working father, of all my heartbroken mamas & dads.

WHO WILL LIVE to write The Role of Moonlight in the Evolution of Consciousness?

IN NEW YORK, San Francisco & points in between the sad young men & women are packaging their wounds & hawking them; braggadocios cleansing old blood from syringes & sly needles in preparation for fresh offerings of cold hard chemical bliss: ofays wasted on suburban plenitude; not-together Bloods strung out on dreams.

I'M OUT HERE alone, off to one side, in the soft dark inspecting a stripe of tree shadow on my moonlit hand, dissolving into mineral light, quivering donkey light, the waters churning with fish & flora, happiness circulating thru my nervous system like island galaxies thru space.

•

MEXICO CAN BE Moon can be Madness can be Maya. But the rising notion that we are in the process of evolving from ape to angel under the influence of star-gazing is the Dream.

Dear Old Stockholm

Of course it is snowing
but two city girls,
one blonde the other black-
haired, are preparing for bed
in a warm apartment they share.
One is washing her hair in the bathroom sink
while the other does hatha yoga exercises.
They have been dancing with some young men
who spoke nothing but north american english,
one of them from Pittsburgh
(from Crawford's Grill up on the Hill)
& the other
a fingerpopper from Leamington, Ontario.

Suddenly, recalling the evening,
the rushing from taxis up inside music clubs,
all of them pleased that it should be so,
the bathroom blonde
who,
like a great many scandinavians,
played some instrument in secondary school
whistles John Coltrane's whole solo
from the Miles Davis *Dear Old Stockholm*
which had been an old swedish folk song.
In fluorescent abandon

& in time
she massages her foamy scalp
with delight.

The young black-haired woman,
hearing all this
—tensed in a shoulderstand,
head full of new blood,
filling with new breath—
is overcome with unexpected happiness.

Each girl smiles in private
at the joyfullness of the evening
& at the music & the men, wishing
it would never end

The apples are still as sweet
as the loquats are plentiful
& the breeze thru both trees
sings promises to me
that the sky reinforces

Like sailors of old
I too am amply tattoo'd
with pictures from a journey
thru lives the yogis say
I myself quite consciously chose

before returning to this planet
to work out hassles
Ive sometimes evaded evenings
with a tilt of the beercan
or the clicking on of music

Inside my skin I am intact
striving to be sweeter to the taste
than apple or loquat or wind
itself. My goals havent changed.
Mingus once said, "Youve probably

written the same way for a million years."

My heart is more tattoo'd than skin
but the wrinkles you see & white hairs
are designs, records, roadmaps
into a region vaster & deeper than

Marlboro Country, an orchard
where harvest isnt always sweet,
a funnytime land of suns & moons
whose only citizen gets lost enough
to signal irreverently for help

THE MOVE CONTINUING

Continuing

for Jim & Jeanie Houston

Take time as lubricant or
time as deterrent, it can
either oil my gears or stop
me right here in my tracks for
snow or grass to cover up.

Green leaves, red leaves, fallen leaves
—a matter of time, distance,
room for change to happen in.
Death's as much a happening
as birth, a process, a move,
a moving forth always, the
end never in sight except
perhaps to the gifted blind.

How much distance does the heart
cover in one lifetime of
beating? How much love is killed
in its final wising up
to the sad ways of the world?

If Ive ignored time for months
in order to concentrate
on getting by & basics,
it's because a light within
me that once flashed red or green
is gradually yellowing,
casually mellowing me
for lifetimes of vigilance.

Only parts of the pain of living
may be captured in a poem or
tale or song or in the image seen.

Even in life we only halfway feel
the tears of a brother or sister,
mass disenchantment in cities,
our discovery of love's meagerness,
the slow rise and fall of the sun.

Sadness is the theme of existence;
joy its variations. Pain is only a portion
of sadness, and efforts to escape it
can lead to self-destruction,
one aspect of pain lived imaginatively.

It is in life that we celebrate pain;
It is in art that we imitate it.

Beauty is saddening, or, as the man sings,
"The bitter note makes the song so sweet."

Maya

The life I've led keeps me from committing suicide . . .

Blaise Cendrars

Songbirds gigging all across California
zipping past slowed-down lenses of the waking eye
dont know this bird
a softer bird
a bird me more than shadows I cast
the moon tonight
as fat as a goose
flashing all thru me
funnybird that zooms
like a feeling
straight up
to escape the heart's net
winging
        winging
                further yet
even beyond tantrums
the world throws
aimed at crippling creatures in flight

Sweet tourists of the soul
there never flew a cockatoo

there never was a tiger cub
there never was an antelope
that leaped or dove
more longingly than I
for love
up into that clean white sky
of the eye's mind

There never lived an Asian brother
or Bantu lover
or Cherokee
whose love of floating surpassed my own

Merciful Kali
Bringer & Taker-Away of feathers & bricks
bring me to the true & lasting route to joyfulness
that I may forsake
the use of filthy drugs
& not misuse this gift of speech

Identities

So youre playing
Macbeth in Singapore
1937 before you were
even born perhaps

The lady is warm,
your lines are waiting
in your stomach
to be heard.

An old seacoast drunk
in pullover blue cap
stomps up one-legged
onto the stage to
tell you youve got no
business playing this
bloody Macbeth,
not a lonely black boy
like you, lost like
himself in a new world
where it's no longer
a matter of whom
thou knowest so much
as it is who you know.

(Say the lady warming
is a career bohemian
with OK looks & a
Vassar education)

Say the future seems
fractured in view of
the worsening wars
in Europe & Asia &
the old man's just
shattered your last
chance illusion.

Well, do you go on
& Shakespeare anyway
or reach for the sky
for the 500th time?

for Arlin J.

My beautiful wife
of the flower nights,
as we sail together
the dawns of consciousness
into days of the sun
from warmed over moons
of our darknesses,

keep in starry memory
how heaven has loaned us
one to the other
long enough only
that each might surrender
nothing that was not once
everything to either
in the lazy waste
of self-indulgence

(& just what could we share
that wouldnt just serve
to reward one's self
or no one?).

Merging like months
to form these years,

light that once blinded
now dazzles us.

You so clearly serve me
in all that you give
that I am ashamed
when I only flash back
thru clouds
my emerging love.

Squirrels

Squirrels are skittering
outside thru the trees
of my bedroom window,
laying it on the line
of my consciousness

Brown & black, furry &
scurrying, how can I not
help loving them like
an old bopster loves licks
laid down building up
so many beats to the moment?

Squirrels may be crazy
but they arent dullards
They like to play too
They cant be hustling nuts &
hoard all the time. Like
everybody else they love
a good chase now & again

Swishing thru branch leaves,
drumming on my diamond roof,
the shining young squirrels
are making & saving the day

for Peter Beagle

There is a sadness to this world

There is a grimness
a nastiness in the throat
a foulness of breath
a slackening of the penis into sorrow
a chill in the bloodstream that hurts
—limitations of fleshhood!
   pain of becoming!
In a spasm of forgetfulness
the seed is sown

There is a ragged edge of my life
a shabby contour
rounding down into nowhere,
the rainyness of wanting
I might well have known
wrestling by the woodstove
in Red Clay Mississippi

There is a tumbling
from noplace to noplace
& there is a crumbling
from nothing to zero,
a journey from germ to germ again
in which the soul travels nowhere

There is such thing as soul,
I have felt it & can feel it moving
within myself & others
in spite of ourselves,
the stolen landscapes we frequent
the caverns of doubt in which we hide

There is such thing as life &
it is not this bleak intermission
during which I scurry for bread & lodging
or judge myself by my failures

O there is a shadowy side of my house
where old dreams harbor
where longings go up in smoke
where a cold & ugly opposite of love
is burning under the sun

Yes brothers you invented jazz
& now I'm inventing myself
as lean & prone to deviance
as the brilliance of your
musical utterance, a wind
that sweeps again & again
thru my American window

What a life you sent me
running out into expecting
everyone to know at once
just what it was I was
talking or not talking about

The genius of our race
has far from run its course
& if the rhythms & melody
I lay down this long street
to paradise arent concrete
enough it can only be because
lately Ive grown used to taking
a cozier route than that of
my contemporary ancestors

Where you once walked or ran
or railroaded your way thru
I now fly, caressing the sturdy
air with balls of my feet
flapping my arms & zeroing

Stay beautiful
but dont stay down underground too long
Dont turn into a mole
or a worm
or a root
or a stone

Come on out into the sunlight
Breathe in trees
Knock out mountains
Commune with snakes
& be the very hero of birds

Dont forget to poke your head up
& blink
Think
Walk all around
Swim upstream

Dont forget to fly

The Move Continuing

All beginnings start right here.
The suns & moons of our spirit
keep touching.
I look out the window at rain
& listen casually to latest developments
of the apocalypse
over the radio
barely unpacked &
hear you shuttling in the backgrounds
from one end of the new apartment
to the other
bumping into boxes of personal belongings
I cant remember having touched 48 hours ago.
Jazz
a very ancient music
whirls beneficently
into our rented front room.

I grow back thru years
to come upon myself
shivering
in my own presence of long ago
when the bittersweet world
passed before
(rather than thru)
me

a vibrant collage
of delights
in supercolor.

It wasnt difficult becoming a gypsy.
At one end of the line
there was God.
& at the very other end
there is God.
In between
shine all the stars of all the spaces
illuminating everything
from the two tender points
that are your eyes
to the musical instruments
of these strong but gentle black men
glowing on the LP in the dark,
the darkness of my own heart
beating its way along
thru all the evenings
that lengthen my skies,
all the stockings
that have ever been rolled down
sadly,
lover & beloved
reaching
to touch one another
at this different time
in this different place
as tho tonight were only the beginning
of all those
yester-
days